A Musical

Book by

ROBERT THOMAS NOLL

Music by

DAVID POGUE

Lyrics by

ROBERT THOMAS NOLL and DAVID POGUE

**Dramatic Publishing**

Woodstock, Illinois • England • Australia • New Zealand

(CIRCUS TIME!)

ISBN: 1-58342-287-0

## IMPORTANT BILLING AND CREDIT REQUIREMENTS

All producers of the Musical *must* give credit to the Author and Composer of the Musical in all programs distributed in connection with performances of the Musical and in all instances in which the title of the Musical appears for purposes of advertising, publicizing or otherwise exploiting the Musical and/or a production. The names of the author and Composer *must* also appear on a separate line, on which no other name appears, immediately following the title, and *must* appear in size of type not less than fifty percent (50%.) the size of the title type. Biographical information on the Author and Composer, if included in the playbook, may be used in all programs. *In all programs this notice must appear:*

"Produced by special arrangement with
THE DRAMATIC PUBLISHING COMPANY of Woodstock, Illinois"

CIRCUS TIME! had its world premiere at The Cleveland Play House on April 8, 1982, with the following cast:

Joey . . . . . . . . . . . . . . . . . . . . . . . . . . . . . . . Leon Adato
Mother's Voice . . . . . . . . . . . . . . . . . . . . . Cassandra Wolfe
Ringmaster . . . . . . . . . . . . . . . . . . . . . . . . . . . David Natale
Fearless Freddie Fangoonee . . . . . . . . . Robby Leatherman
Jeanelle . . . . . . . . . . . . . . . . . . . . . . . . . . . Juli Ann Davis
Ellie . . . . . . . . . . . . . . . . . . . . . . . . . . . . . . Judy Crozier
Nellie . . . . . . . . . . . . . . . . . . . . . . . . . . . Shawn Scheuer
Alison . . . . . . . . . . . . . . . . . . . . . . . . . . . . . Leah Natale
Amazing Alan . . . . . . . . . . . . . . . . . . . Andrew C. Watson
Clowns . . . Erin Branagan, Laura Meckler, Maura Murphy,
Amy Notley, Daniele O'Loughlin, Lee Unkrich

Director . . . . . . . . . . . Kerro Knox 3 and Elisabeth Farwell
Choreograper . . . . . . . . . . . . . . . . . . . . Elisabeth Farwell
Music Director . . . . . . . . . . . . . . . . . . . . . . David Wolfson
Costume Designer . . . . . . . . . . . . . . . . . . . Betsy Streeter
Lighting Designer . . . . . . . . . . . . . . . . . . . . Paul K. Wells
Magic Advisor . . . . . . . . . . . . . . . . . . . . . . Aaron Watkins
Properties . . . . . . . . . . . . . . . . . . . . . . . . . . James A. Guy
Stage Manager . . . . . . . . . . . . . . . . . . . . . . Rhona Nathan
Follow Spot . . . . . . . . . . . . . . . . . . . . . . . . . . Homer Farr
Cleveland Play House Artistic Director . . . Richard Oberlin
Director of The Play House Youtheatre . . Cassandra Wolfe

# CIRCUS TIME!

A Musical in One Act

CHARACTERS

JOEY, a young boy
JOEY'S OFFSTAGE MOTHER
RINGMASTER
FEARLESS FREDDIE FANGOONEE, high-wire artist
JEANELLE, the elephant
ELLIE, her sister
NELLIE, her other sister
AMAZING ALAN, magician
ALISON, his assistant

CIRCUS CLOWN #1
CLOWN #2
CLOWN #3
CLOWN #4
CLOWN #5
CLOWN #6
(You can have as many clowns as you want.)

The ENSEMBLE is made up of the CLOWNS, plus, a LION, a LION TAMER, and maybe a BEARDED LADY, a STILT WALKER, HORSES, TIGERS, JUGGLERS, TRAPEZE ARTISTS, etc.

The ENSEMBLE backs up the singers throughout the production.

## MUSICAL NUMBERS

"Circus Time!" . . . . . . . . . . . . . Ringmaster and Company

"I'm Scared" . . . . . . . . . . . . . . . . . . . . . . . Freddie and Joey

"Elephants Sometimes Forget" . . . . . . . . . . . . . . . . Jeanelle

"Your Own Beat" . . . . . . . . . . . . . Joey, Jeanelle, Company

"Magic" . . . . . . . . . . . . . . . . . . . . . . . . . . . Alan and Alison

"Make You Laugh" . . . . . . . . . . . . Joey, Clowns, Company

"Farewell/Circus Time! Reprise". . Ringmaster, Joey, Company

# CIRCUS TIME!

SETTING: *Joey's bedroom. His bed is unmade. His bathrobe lies on the floor beneath its hook. His toys—a set of circus dolls and several stuffed animals are arranged on the floor.*

AT RISE: *JOEY is playing with his circus toys.*

MOTHER *(offstage)*. Joey, are you cleaning your room?

JOEY *(reluctantly)*. Yes, Mom.

MOTHER *(offstage, always pleasant)*. We'll be having dinner soon. That room better be clean.

JOEY. Yes, Mom.

MOTHER *(offstage)*. Put your toys away. Make your bed. And hang up your bathrobe.

JOEY. Yes, Mom. *(Throws his bathrobe on the hook. It falls to the floor. He doesn't bother. Instead of picking it up, he goes back to playing with his circus toys.)* In the circus nobody has to work. The clowns laugh. The animals dance. The trapeze artist flies through the air. And everybody has a great time! If I was in the circus... *(Picks up the ringmaster doll.)* All right, Ringmaster! Line up all the acts. We're ready to start the circus parade! Lion tamer, trapeze artist, bearded lady, elephants, a magician, tigers, and, of course, the clowns. *(Starts moving the dolls around the floor as he imitates an old circus pipe organ. He starts singing the "traditional" circus theme music:)* "Da…da…da-da-da-da-da-da…"

**(SONG #1: "CIRCUS TIME!")**

*(Hear circus train whistle. As JOEY continues to sing like a circus pipe organ, a real one is heard—possibly on tape. The music gets louder and louder and brighter and brighter. Hearing real circus music surprises JOEY.)*

JOEY. What's happening? *(Pointing down the theater aisle or upstage behind him.)* And over there! Look what's coming!

*(Actors dressed as circus performers enter. They are lead by the RINGMASTER.)*

CIRCUS ENSEMBLE *(singing).*

**CATCH THE TUNE.**
**FEEL THE BEAT.**
**IT'S THE CIRCUS PARADE**
**COMIN' DOWN THE STREET.**
**HANG ON TO YOUR HATS**
**FOR A THREE-RING SHOW—**
**THIS SPECTACULAR DAY**
**IS ALL FOR JOE.**

JOEY *(speaking under music).* For me? *(JOEY sees that his circus toys and stuffed animals have vanished.)* Look! My circus toys have come alive!

*(As they sing, the ENSEMBLE builds the circus area right in the middle of Joey's bedroom. Now that the cir-*

*cus has arrived, we should see the circus risers upstage angled in a semicircle; colorful circus banners can be brought in or flown in. When the ENSEMBLE is not "on stage," the ENSEMBLE should be seated on the risers. They become part of the circus audience. They also serve as the play's stage crew and they back up the singers throughout the production.)*

ALL.

**STEP RIGHT UP—DON'T BE SHY**
**WE'LL MAKE SMILES APPEAR**
**AND CAUSE SPIRITS TO FLY.**
**WE'LL BUILD AN ILLUSION**
**OR TWO OR THREE**
**YOU'LL BE GLUED TO YOUR SEAT**
**JUST WAIT AND SEE.**

RINGMASTER.

**YOU'LL SEE...**
**ELEGANT ELEPHANTS DANCING**
**STUNNING WHITE STALLIONS PRANCING**
**LIONS AND TIGERS ROARING**
**MEN ON THE HIGH TRAPEZE SOARING.**

ALL.

**IT'S CIRCUS TIME FOR JOEY.**
**WE'RE HERE AT YOUR COMMAND**
**ONE, TWO, THREE**
**AND WE'RE READY TO**
**STRIKE UP THE BAND.**
**IT'S CIRCUS TIME FOR JOEY.**
**WITH WIZARDRY TO DO.**
**DON'T YOU SEE**
**WE ARE RUNNING AWAY TO JOIN YOU.**

**CATCH THE TUNE**
**FEEL THE BEAT**
**IT'S THE CIRCUS PARADE**
**COMIN' DOWN THE STREET.**
**HANG ON TO YOUR HATS**
**FOR A THREE-RING SHOW**
**THIS SPECTACULAR DAY**
**IS ALL FOR JOE.**

RINGMASTER.
**YOU'LL SEE**
**COMICAL CLOWNS AND ACROBATS**
**MYSTICAL MAGIC AND BIG CATS.**
**COURAGE AND TALENT**
**AND SOME SPILLS**
**FIRE AND DAZZLE**
**AND NEAT THRILLS.**

JOEY. My very own circus!

RINGMASTER. Yes, Joey's Circus.

JOEY. How many rings?

RINGMASTER. How many do you want?

JOEY. Three… A three-ring circus!

RINGMASTER. You want three. Okay, a three-ring circus is coming right up. You want three rings?

JOEY. Yes.

RINGMASTER. Then you'll have your three rings… *(Magically takes out three large rings and hands them to JOEY.)* One, two, three.

JOEY. Wow! My own three-ring circus! *(Puts the rings down on the stage.)*

ALL *(singing).*

**IF YOU'LL BELIEVE IN MAGIC**
**IF YOU WILL COME OUR WAY**
**YOU WILL JOIN US—**
**IT'S CIRCUS TIME TODAY!**

*(The entire ENSEMBLE bow and then take their seats upstage on the risers. JOEY and RINGMASTER move downstage.)*

JOEY. Now, Mister Ringmaster, let's begin the show! Let's start with one of your top acts, please. A real showstopper!

RINGMASTER. Anything you wish, you're the B-O-S-S. *(Hands JOEY a hat with a large "Boss" on it.)*

JOEY. I'm the B-O-S-S. I'm in charge.

RINGMASTER. You're in charge.

JOEY. What do I do now?

RINGMASTER. I don't know, you're the B-O-S-S. How about giving some orders?

JOEY. Right. I'll give some orders. *(Looking puzzled.)* What kind of orders?

RINGMASTER. May I make a suggestion, B-O-S-S?

JOEY. Sure.

RINGMASTER. How about telling me, your faithful Ringmaster, to start the show?

JOEY. Good idea. Thanks. *(To ENSEMBLE.)* All right, all you members of Joey's world-famous circus, let the fun begin! Announce the first act, Ringmaster.

RINGMASTER. Right away, sir. *(RINGMASTER moves DC into darkness.)* Hey, a…spotlight, please! *(Spotlight is R area.)* No, I'm over here. *(Spotlight moves to L area.)* No, I'm over here! Here! *(Spotlight moves to R area again. RINGMASTER jumps up and down in frustration. Waving hands.)* I'm right here! Right here! *(Spotlight moves to JOEY.)*

JOEY. I'm not the Ringmaster. *(Proudly.)* I'm the owner. I'm the—

ENSEMBLE *(in unison)*. B-O-S-S, we know.

RINGMASTER *(waving hands like crazy)*. Joey, help me!

JOEY. Help you. How can I…? *(Gets an idea. JOEY moves DCR next to the RINGMASTER. The spotlight follows him.)*

RINGMASTER *(basking in the spotlight)*. Oh, finally. Thanks.

JOEY. No problem…

RINGMASTER *(to audience, regaining his composure)*. Now, ladies and gentlemen, in the center ring, Joey's world-famous circus is proud to present the incredible, the fabulous, the breathtaking, the stupendous…

JOEY *(to audience, rubbing his hands)*. Gee, this ought to be something, eh?

RINGMASTER. …The Fearless Freddie Fangoonee, Artist Extraordinaire of the High Wire...

*(Lights come up on the "high wire" which is a long stick on the floor; no one is there.)*

RINGMASTER *(louder, looking and shouting offstage)*. …On the high wire the fabulous…the remarkable master of Balance and Nerve, Fearless Fangoonee. *(Still no one is there.)* Excuse me.

*(RINGMASTER moves into wings. JOEY gives audience a perplexed look.)*

RINGMASTER *(yelling offstage)*. Fearless Fangoonee, get your rear-end over here! Freddie, get your body on to that high wire right now!

*(Moves to ENSEMBLE on upstage risers.)*

CLOWN #1. Fearless isn't here.
CLOWN #2. We don't know where he went.
CLOWN #3. We haven't seen him.
CLOWN #4. He's not here. Sorry. *(RINGMASTER storms off.)*
JOEY *(to audience)*. Just what kind of circus do we have here? I'm beginning to wonder.

*(RINGMASTER quickly reenters and starts pacing.)*

RINGMASTER. Joey, maybe you can help me. Have you seen a little man wearing yellow leotards?
JOEY. Well... *(Starts looking around stage and sees a pair of purple shoes visible under one of the circus banners.)* Have I seen a little man wearing yellow leotards and purple shoes?

*(JOEY looks behind banner and sees FANGOONEE. FANGOONEE gets on his knees pleading with JOEY to say "No.")*

RINGMASTER. Yes, have you?

*(FANGOONEE makes a large "no" motion with his head shaking vigorously.)*

JOEY *(shaking head vigorously).* No. I haven't seen any little guy wearing yellow leotards and purple shoes. And red trunks.

RINGMASTER. Oh, circus feathers! I wonder where that little runt went? *(Moving into audience.)* Boys and girls, have you seen a little guy wearing yellow leotards, purple shoes and red trunks hiding? Have you?

*(FANGOONEE gets on his knees and pleads with the audience to say "no." He shakes his head vigorously. FANGOONEE pleads with parents—adults—to say "no" too.)*

RINGMASTER. Well, there's only one other place to look. I'll be right back. I bet he's in the bathroom.

*(RINGMASTER goes down the aisle into the lobby. FANGOONEE notices JOEY and audience looking at him. He comes from behind banner.)*

FANGOONEE. All clear. *(Moves to JOEY.)* Thanks a lot, Joey. Pleased to meet you. *(JOEY shakes FANGOONEE's hand as FANGOONEE's glove comes off and into JOEY's hand.)*

JOEY. Pleased to meet you. *(Hands FANGOONEE back his glove.)*

FANGOONEE. Thanks. *(To JOEY and audience.)* You're probably wondering why I'm not up on the high wire thrilling you all, huh? Huh?

JOEY. Well…

FANGOONEE *(looking at children in audience)*. Yes, I see that wondering look in your eyes.

JOEY. Well, the Ringmaster did call you "the incredible, the fabulous, the breathtaking, the stupendous, remarkable…

FANGOONEE. Yes, stupendously remarkable.

JOEY. …Master of Balance and Nerve."

FANGOONEE *(disgustedly with his head down)*. Balance and Nerve, huh!

JOEY. And brave and courageous.

FANGOONEE. But I'm not brave, I'm not courageous. I'm frightened. I'm scared to death.

JOEY. I don't believe that.

FANGOONEE. Believe it. I used to be the best—my act *was* thrilling. I could do cartwheels and somersaults on the high wire. I could ride a bicycle or a tricycle, or juggle—I could even stand on my head—

JOEY. Way up high in the sky.

FANGOONEE. Hundreds of feet above, with no net.

JOEY. That *is* fearless.

FANGOONEE. How the audience would ooh…

ENSEMBLE *(looking up and pointing)*. Ooh…

FANGOONEE. And ahh.

ENSEMBLE. Ahh…

FANGOONEE. They would clap and cheer. *(ENSEMBLE claps and then cheers.)*

JOEY. Then what happened?

FANGOONEE. Then one day, for the first time in my life, I made a big mistake. *(ENSEMBLE dramatically gasps in unison.)* A big, big, big mistake.

JOEY. What did you do?

FANGOONEE. Something I never did in all my years on the high wire.

JOEY. What?

FANGOONEE. I looked down. *(ENSEMBLE groans.)* I suddenly realized where I was…hundreds of feet up in the air without a net. And from that day on… *(Stops.)*

JOEY. From that day on, what?

FANGOONEE. Joey, I can't hide it any longer.

*(Music starts.)*

JOEY. You can't hide what?

FANGOONEE. My fear.

JOEY. Fear?

FANGOONEE. My fear of heights. *(Sings.)*

**(SONG #2: "I'M SCARED")**

**I'M SCARED! I'M SCARED! I'M SCARED!**
**JUST THE THOUGHT OF IT**
**CAN MAKE ME START TO CRY.**
**THOUGH OTHER MEN HAVE DARED**
**TO TIPTOE THROUGH THE SKY,**
**I'M SCARED.**

**I WASN'T REALLY CUT OUT FOR THE HIGH WIRE.**
**THE TELEPHONE'S A LITTLE MORE**
**LIKE MY WIRE.**
**I'M PETRIFIED OF HEIGHTS.**
**JUST TO LOOK AT IT AND I BEGIN TO DOUBT**
**YOU WANT YOUR NAME IN LIGHTS?**
**NOT ME—I'VE CHICKENED OUT!**

*(ENSEMBLE might all for a few seconds move their bodies like chickens.)*

FANGOONEE.

**A LONG TIME AGO I WOULD GALLANTLY SHOW**
**ALL THE WORLD WHAT A TALENT I WAS.**
**A MARVEL INDEED,**
**ANY TRICK WOULD SUCCEED,**
**BUT I'M GROUNDED NOW'DAYS BECAUSE**
**I'M SCARED! I'M SCARED! I'M SCARED!**
**IF YOU LOVE ME YOU WILL**
**HIDE ME FROM THE SIGHT.**
**NO TIGHTROPE STAR HAS SHARED**
**THIS AWFUL FEAR OF HEIGHTS.**
**I'M SCARED!**

*(Under music.)*

It must be that Freddie Fangoonee has gotten too old.

JOEY. You don't look very old.

FANGOONEE. Well, I am.

JOEY. How old are you, may I ask?

FANGOONEE. Count the wrinkles under my eyes. Look at the gray hairs that I have. See the stiffness creeping in my fingers!

JOEY. You look fine to me.

FANGOONEE. No, old age has set in. I'm looking for my rocker and shawl…

JOEY. How old *are* you?

FANGOONEE. I'll be twenty-eight in June.

JOEY. My, you are getting up there. But you're not *too* old.

FANGOONEE. I'm not?

JOEY. Now, my father, he's thirty-two. Now that's old.

FANGOONEE. Then I have a few years left?

JOEY. You sure do. You have lots of years left to perform on the tightrope. Now, come on…climb that ladder in the center ring and do your act. We're all waiting.

*(ENSEMBLE ad lib encouragement.)*

FANGOONEE *(to JOEY, then to ENSEMBLE)*. But, I told you that I'm…

JOEY & ENSEMBLE. We know. We know.

JOEY *(singing)*.

**YOU'RE SCARED! YOU'RE SCARED! YOU'RE SCARED!**
**BUT I DON'T THINK IT'S AS**
**AWFUL AS IT SEEMS.**
**FOR WITH ME, YOU SEE, YOU'VE SHARED**
**ALL YOUR SECRETS, HOPES AND DREAMS**
**BUT NOW—**
**IF STARDOM LURES YOU**
**LET ME HELP YOU GET THERE:**
**YOU WON'T BE SCARED**
**IF YOU'LL JUST PUT A NET THERE!**

FANGOONEE.

**A NET! A NET! A NET!**
**JUST WHAT KIND OF CHEAPSKATE**
**DO YOU THINK I AM?**
**MY PRIDE WOULD SOON REGRET**
**THIS POOR AND CHILDISH PLAN.**

JOEY.

**BUT, FREDDIE, A NET THERE**
**WILL HELP YOU FORGET**
**HOW DANG'ROUSLY LOFTY YOU ARE.**
**TO HELP YOU UNWIND**
**YOU SHOULD KEEP WELL IN MIND**
**THAT SOMEDAY YOU MIGHT BE…**

FANGOONEE *(getting the idea).*

**A STAR!**

*(ENSEMBLE applauds and cheers. JOEY directs members of the ENSEMBLE to place a net under the high wire. FANGOONEE "climbs" to the "high" wire and begins to perform. He even looks down.)*

FANGOONEE.

**I'M CURED! I'M CURED! I'M CURED!**
**AND I'M HAPPY AS A GUY COULD EVER BE**
**ONE MORE CRISIS I'VE ENDURED.**
**JUST BY THINKING LOGIC'LLY,**
**I'M CURED!**
**I FEEL AS SAFE AS ANY SHIP IN HARBOR**
**FROM NOW ON I'LL GET "CLOSE SHAVES"**
**AT THE BARBER.**

**I'M BOLD! I'M BOLD! I'M BOLD!**
**TO THE THUNDEROUS APPLAUSE**
**OF ONE AND ALL.**
**I'M GETTING KIND OF OLD BUT I'M OKAY.**
**IF I…SHOULD…**

*(A little too daring, he loses is balance and falls onto the net, springs back up, smiling.)*

FANGOONEE.
**FALL!!!**

*(FANGOONEE, all smiles, is again walking the tightrope. He may do a somersault or other trick. RINGMASTER excitedly reenters stage applauding.)*

RINGMASTER. Fangoonee! You've done it!

JOEY *(to RINGMASTER)*. You know, I think he's more afraid of getting a few gray hairs than performing on the high wire.

RINGMASTER. You might be right. The important thing, Joey, is you got him back up there.

*(FANGOONEE does a final trick. He bows to ENSEMBLE, then to the audience. He happily exits. Spotlight comes up on RINGMASTER downstage.)*

RINGMASTER. And now, ladies and gentlemen, in the right corner ring, Joey's world-famous circus is proud to present those amazing damsels of dance, those prized and pretty pachyderms, Ellie, Nellie and Jeanelle, the Elephant Sisters!

*(JEANELLE, ELLIE and NELLIE do a soft-shoe tap-dance number in step. This is the dance portion of the song "Your Own Beat." Perhaps tympani can "boom" to the footsteps/dance steps of the elephants' dance. The problem with this dance is that JEANELLE is not in step with her sisters. She keeps missing steps. Finally, ELLIE and NELLIE, her two temperamental sisters, bump her off the stage. They finish their precision dance and bow.*

*ENSEMBLE gives them a rousing cheer as ELLIE and NELLIE exit. JEANELLE, on the floor, is blubbering, crying her heart out. JOEY moves to her.)*

JOEY. Hello, there. *(JEANELLE ignores him and just keeps crying.)* Hi. *(JEANELLE continues to cry.)* I'm Joey…the…

JEANELLE. I know…you're the B-O-S-S-E, the boss.

JOEY. It's spelled B-O-S-S, there's no "E" at the end.

JEANELLE *(cries even louder)*. Oh, I can't get anything right. I bet you came here to fire me, right? I won't give you any trouble—I'll go quietly.

*(JEANELLE is having a hard time getting up from the floor. Some of the CLOWNS give her a hand to help her up. She starts to leave.)*

JOEY. No, Jeanelle, no. Don't go!

JEANELLE. You mean you're not going to give me to some zoo, where all I'll do all day is eat grass and look at people. Have little kids throw peanuts at me? I don't like peanuts. And I especially don't like the taste of the shells. *(Sniffs with her trunk.)* I do like peanut butter and jelly sandwiches, though.

JOEY. You do? I'll have to remember that at feeding time.

JEANELLE *(crying)*. Oh, I'm such a strange elephant.

JOEY. No, you're not.

JEANELLE. Yes, I am. I'm weird! Weird! Weird!

*(JEANELLE starts crying again. JOEY takes a small handkerchief from his pocket.)*

JOEY. No, you're not, Jeanelle. You're just different. Here, wipe your tears.

JEANELLE. Thank you.

*(JEANELLE takes the small hankie and opens it, it keeps getting bigger and bigger. She loudly blows her nose, HONK SOUND—hopefully a sound effect from someone in ENSEMBLE, with such force that JOEY is blown away to the other side of the stage. Maybe some ENSEMBLE members are also blown away with him. JOEY falls on his rear. CRASH SOUND—again, maybe provided live by someone in the upstage ENSEMBLE.)*

JEANELLE. Oh, I'm sorry. I didn't mean to… Now I've given you another reason to fire me. Go on, what zoo are you shipping me to?

JOEY. Take it easy, big girl; I'm not going to fire you.

JEANELLE. You know, I try so hard to learn my steps. I rehearse with my sisters every day…and I practice all the time on my own. But, I've ruined the girls' act. They won't speak to me. They hate me. My own sisters hate me.

JOEY. No, Jeanelle, I'm sure they don't hate you.

JEANELLE. Yes they do.

*(JEANELLE cries again and begins to blow her nose. JOEY is again blown to the other side of the stage. Again, maybe some members of the ENSEMBLE are also blown to the other side with him.)*

JEANELLE *(starts practicing her dance steps)*. You see, even though I practice my steps morning, noon and night, I know the steps, but I can't remember what order they're in. I am just one dumb dumb elephant.

JOEY. But, I always thought elephants never forget.

JEANELLE. Well… *(Singing slowly and melodramatically.)*

**(SONG #3: "ELEPHANTS SOMETIMES FORGET")**

**JOEY, MY FRIEND**
**I THINK THIS IS THE END**
**OF MY JOURNEY WITH THE CIRCUS;**
**WE'LL NEVER SUCCEED**
**I'M A FAILURE INDEED,**
**NO MATTER HOW THEY WORK US.**
**I TRIP ON THE TANGO**
**AND WILT ON THE WALTZ**
**WHEN THEY DO THE SAMBA**
**I DO SOMERSAULTS.**

**LET ME TELL YOU THIS**
**THE REASON I DO THIS**
**AND MANGLE EACH MINUET—**
**AS A DODO BIRD DANCER**
**I'LL TELL YOU THE ANSWER**
**ELEPHANTS SOMETIMES FORGET!**

*(In tempo, lumbering waltz.)*

**ONE, TWO, THREE, ONE, TWO, THREE,**
**LOOK AT ME**
**I AM NOT TOO BRIGHT,**
**FOUR, FIVE, SIX, FOUR, FIVE, SIX,**
**NO NEW TRICKS**
**'TIL I GET IT RIGHT.**

**I CAN'T REMEMBER**
**THE STEPS I SHOULD TAKE**
**THEY MAKE THE BIG TIME**
**AND I MAKE MISTAKES.**
**DID THEY SAY I TAP**
**THE HEEL OR THE TOE?**
**ALL I GET IS UPTIGHT**
**AND UPSET.**
**WHICH GOES TO SHOW**
**AS THE SAYING SHOULD GO:**
**ELEPHANTS SOMETIMES FORGET.**

**I'M ALWAYS OFF A BEAT**
**MAKING US INCOMPLETE**
**I HAVE GOT FOUR LEFT FEET**
**WHAT WILL I DO?**
**DANCE STEPS ESCAPE ME**
**MY SISTERS HATE ME**
**THEY WANT TO CRATE ME**
**BACK TO THE ZOO.**

*(JEANELLE tries to dance. She gets her legs twisted and falls to floor with a LOUD THUD. Maybe have the ENSEMBLE dance together behind her without making any mistakes.)*

JEANELLE.
**I HAVE GOOD INTENTIONS**
**BUT I HAVE HORRIBLE RETENTION**
**OF THE STEPS**
**AND NOT TO MENTION**
**I HAVE ACID INDIGESTION.**
*(Burps, under music.)*
Have you ever heard an elephant burp? *(Sings.)*

**I AM A THREAT**
**TO A DAZZLING DUET**
**'CAUSE MY MEMORY TENDS TO ROAM**
**THEY GET UPSET**
**EV'RY TIME I FORGET,**
**I THINK I'LL PACK**
**MY TRUNK AND GO HOME.**
**ONE, TWO, THREE, ONE, TWO, THREE,**
**LOOK AT ME**
**I AM NOT TOO BRIGHT.**
**FOUR, FIVE, SIX, FOUR, FIVE, SIX,**
**NO NEW TRICKS**
**'TIL I GET IT RIGHT.**

**I CAN'T REMEMBER**
**THE STEPS I SHOULD TAKE**
**THEY MAKE THE BIG TIME**
**AND I MAKE MISTAKES.**
**DID THEY SAY I TAP**
**THE HEEL OR THE TOE?**
**ALL I GET IS UPTIGHT AND UPSET**
**WHICH GOES TO SHOW,**
**AS THE SAYING SHOULD GO:**
**ELEPHANTS SOMETIMES FORGET.**

*(ELLIE and NELLIE reenter crossing the stage and laughing at JEANELLE.)*

ELLIE. Hey, look at Dumbo there!
NELLIE. Forget your steps again, peanut brain?
JOEY. Come on, don't be mean, girls. Where are you going?
ELLIE. We can't dance with this two-ton toddler.
NELLIE. Yes, she has ruined our act for the final time.

*(ELLIE and NELLIE turn up their trunks toward JEANELLE as they snootily exit. JEANELLE starts crying again. She reaches for handkerchief. JOEY and members of the ENSEMBLE quickly brace themselves for the big blow. She dries her eyes with it. JOEY and ENSEMBLE sigh with relief.)*

JOEY. Jeanelle, there has to be some way to make you a dancer. You certainly do try hard.

JEANELLE. I think it's hopeless. I have four left feet.

JOEY. No, you don't.

JEANELLE. I do and you know it. Besides, I never really wanted to be a dancing elephant anyways.

JOEY. You didn't?

JEANELLE. No. I only became one because my sisters did. We all took lessons when we were calves.

JOEY. What did you want to be?

JEANELLE. You really want to know?

JOEY. I really want to know.

JEANELLE. You'll laugh.

JOEY. No, I promise I won't.

JEANELLE. I wanted to be a horse.

JOEY *(fighting back the laughter)*. A horse?

JEANELLE. A horse gets to run all day…she can run and walk and gallop if she likes. She doesn't have to do it in step with anybody. Look at the horses in this show, they don't have to dance together…each one moves in his or her own way to his or her own beat. They're individuals. That's how I want to be. But, I look at me; I can never be a horse no matter how I try. Joey, I hate to do this to you, you seem like a good B-O-S-S, but I'm quitting the circus right now. I'll pick up my trunk and I'll be off.

I've been working for peanuts long enough. Besides, they're so fattening. *(Tearfully starts down the aisle.)* It's been nice knowing you, kid. *(To audience.)* Sorry to disappoint you all. I just wasn't cut out to be part of a sister act.

*(ENSEMBLE ad lib protests as JEANELLE starts to move down the aisle.)*

JOEY *(following her down the aisle)*. Wait! Wait a minute, Jeanelle!

JEANELLE. No, no, too late. I've made up my mind—what little mind I have.

JOEY. But, I have an idea.

JEANELLE *(stops)*. An idea?

JOEY. Jeanelle, how would you like to be like a horse?

JEANELLE. Say again?

JOEY. Like a horse. *(JOEY starts moving like a horse. He makes a horse whinny.)*

JEANELLE. Be like a horse, hmmm…

JOEY. Listen—what does a Ringmaster ride in the circus parade?

JEANELLE. He rides a horse, of course.

JOEY. Jeanelle, from now on I want you to lead the circus parade. The Ringmaster will ride you at the head of the parade. We'll get you a beautiful blanket to wear. You'll look gorgeous. And you'll be so proud. You'll lead the entire parade—and right behind you—your sisters—dancing as a duet.

JEANELLE. To be a duet! That's what they've always wanted. They'll like that.

*(ELLIE and NELLIE reenter.)*

ELLIE. Oh, Jeanelle, Nellie and I are a duet.

NELLIE. No, we'll love that! *(ELLIE and NELLIE as duet, happily dance off.)*

JOEY. And Jeanelle, you'll become a star on your own. Doing what you do best.

JEANELLE. What I do best? Which is…I forgot.

JOEY. You'll dance… *(Sings.)*

**(SONG #4: "YOUR OWN BEAT")**

**TO YOUR OWN BEAT.**
**ON YOUR OWN FEET.**
**YOU CAN IMPROVISE AND KEEP ALL EYES UPON YOU**
**IN YOUR OWN STYLE,**
**FLASH THAT GREAT BIG SMILE,**
**AND YOUR DAYS OF CHORUS DANCING**
**NOW ARE GONE! YOU…**
**WON'T BE WRONG A MINUTE LONGER;**
**EV'RY STEP YOU TAKE**
**WILL BE MUCH SURER AND MUCH STRONGER**
**NEVER A MISTAKE,**
**SO—**

**MARCH TO YOUR OWN DRUMMER;**
**YOU'LL HEAR A DIFF'RENT BEAT,**
**YOU'LL BE THE CIRCUS LEADER,**
**PARADING DOWN THE STREET!**
**DANCE A DIFF'RENT RHYTHM,**
**MARK A DIFF'RENT TIME**
**STAND UP TALL, FOR AFTER ALL,**
**YOU'RE A PACHYDERM IN HER PRIME!**

JEANELLE *(under music)*. A pachyderm in her prime? Hmmm… *(Sings.)*

**I THINK I JUST MIGHT TRY IT, JOEY,**
**DANCING ALL ALONE**
**I NEVER HAVE TRIED SUCH A THING BEFORE**
**I THINK IF I DON'T RUIN IT**
**AND BREAK MY EV'RY BONE,**
**I COULD WIND UP SOLO DANCING EVERMORE!**

*(The music snaps into a two-step during which ELLIE and NELLIE reenter and back up JEANELLE's dance solo.)*

ALL *(to JEANELLE)*.

**MARCH TO YOUR OWN DRUMMER;**
**YOU'LL HEAR A DIFF'RENT BEAT**
**YOU'LL BE THE CIRCUS LEADER,**
**PARADING DOWN THE STREET!**
**DANCE A DIFF'RENT RHYTHM,**
**MARK A DIFF'RENT TIME**
**STAND UP TALL, FOR AFTER ALL,**
**YOU'RE A PACHYDERM IN HER PRIME…**
**A PACHYDERM IN HER PRIME!**

JEANELLE. Oh, thank you, Joey! You've made us girls so happy.

ELLIE & NELLIE. You aren't kidding.

*(JEANELLE gives JOEY a big kiss on the forehead. KISS SOUND done by a member of the ENSEMBLE should sound like a plunger coming off a wall. JEANELLE exits marching to her own drummer.)*

JOEY *(to audience)*. Problem solved. Now, it's time to sit back and relax and enjoy the circus acts. What a terrific day!

RINGMASTER *(entering in a panic)*. What a terrible day!

JOEY. What?

RINGMASTER. Terrible, just terrible.

JOEY. What do you mean? Didn't you see how happy Flying Fangoonee is? I mean, he has his confidence back. And Jeanelle—she can finally dance on her own, and her sisters—

RINGMASTER *(melodramatically)*. Disaster has struck.

ENSEMBLE *(looking all around)*. Where?

RINGMASTER. Disaster.

JOEY. Don't tell me, it's about the next act.

RINGMASTER. Yes, how did you know?

JOEY. Remember who I am, the B-O-S-S…I'm supposed to know everything.

RINGMASTER. Well, then go ahead. You take care of the problem.

JOEY. What problem?

RINGMASTER. I thought you know everything.

JOEY. Maybe I exaggerated a little… What's the problem?

RINGMASTER. The legerdemain…

JOEY. The legerde—what?

RINGMASTER. The legerdemain…gone!

JOEY. Well, can't you get another one from the hardware store?

RINGMASTER. Boy, you really don't know everything. Legerdemain means magic. I'm talking about the circus magician…the Astonishing and Utterly Amazing Alan has disappeared.

JOEY. I knew that magicians make things disappear. I didn't know *they* could disappear.

RINGMASTER. Well, Amazing Alan did. He was talking to me in this very ring here…

*(RINGMASTER moves to ring where ALISON, the magician's assistant, is angrily pacing.)*

RINGMASTER *(continuing)*. …Where Alison, his lovely assistant—

ALISON. And beautiful wife...

RINGMASTER. We were going through the order of his tricks, when all of a sudden…

ALISON. Poof! Alan was gone.

JOEY. Amazing!

ALISON *(angry)*. I've seen him pull this trick before. Every Sunday night when I ask him to take out the garbage, POOF! He's gone.

JOEY. Well, when does he reappear?

ALISON. After I take out the garbage. Poof, he's back. Well, where is he? Amazing Alan! Alan, honey, dear?

RINGMASTER. I told you, Joey, a terrible day. Amazing Alan is one of our most popular acts. All the children will be disappointed. He really is amazing.

ALISON. He's very talented. *(Angry.)* Is he going to get it when he comes home… I won't speak to him!

RINGMASTER. Terrible, terrible!

JOEY. I have an idea.

RINGMASTER. What is it?

JOEY. You don't know what to do…

RINGMASTER. No idea.

JOEY *(motions to ALISON)*. She doesn't know what to do…

ALISON. I know what I'll do when I get my hands on him.

RINGMASTER. But, Joey, I bet you do.

JOEY. Let's ask our friends in the audience for help.

RINGMASTER. Huh?

ALISON. What?

JOEY. Well, what always brings a performer back on stage?

RINGMASTER. Money?

ALISON. An angry wife?

JOEY. An audience. A cheering crowd. And any performer would come back for a standing ovation. *(Goes into audience.)* So come on, boys and girls, moms and dads, grandmas and grandpas, uncles and aunts, cats and dogs, frogs and parakeets…

RINGMASTER. Parakeets?

JOEY. Even people who snuck in. Come on, let's all stand up. Please, come on, all of you!

RINGMASTER *(getting the idea)*. Yes, rise from your seats.

ALISON. Yes, come on. *(Caustically.)* I can't wait to see him.

JOEY. Okay, now everybody, put your hands together and applaud! Come on, everybody—

RINGMASTER. Help us, please.

*(THEATER AUDIENCE applauds. JOEY, RINGMASTER and ALISON motion for them to clap even louder, then: Poof! In a puff of smoke enters AMAZING ALAN. As the*

*applause continues he bows and bows and bows. What a ham!)*

ALAN. Thank you, thank you, thank you...you all must have seen my act before.

ALISON. I've seen this disappearing act before... *(Threatening.)* Wait until we get home...

ALAN. Dearest, please. *(Motions to theater audience.)* Not in front of the children.

ALISON *(to ALAN)*. You left me here all by myself...

ALAN *(dismisses her)*. Sorry. *(To theater audience.)* Now, you may take your seats. Don't want anybody standing in the way of seeing my act.

JOEY *(to theater audience)*. Thank you very much.

RINGMASTER *(to theater audience)*. You made my day not so terrible. Thanks.

ALAN *(motioning to JOEY)*. Who's the kid?

JOEY *(coming up to ALAN)*. I don't believe we've met. I'm Joey, the B-O-S-S.

ALAN. You're a fan of my act?

JOEY. Well, Alan...

ALAN. Please...call me Amazing.

ALISON. He's amazing all right. Amazingly conceited.

JOEY. Would you teach me one of your magic tricks?

ALAN. It takes a lot of practice.

JOEY. I'm willing to work at it... Just tell me how to use a wand. *(Takes one of ALAN's magic wands.)*

ALAN. Hey! Joey, put that down!

JOEY *(moving to an empty cabinet)*. Don't worry; I've seen this trick on TV before.

ALAN. Give me back my magic wand!

JOEY. In a minute. Watch this… All you do is tap this box with this wand like so… *(JOEY starts tapping the cabinet. Unnoticed by JOEY, a LION comes out of it.)* and out comes a little cute cuddly bunny.

*(LION roars. JOEY screams. CHASE MUSIC as LION chases JOEY around stage and maybe into theater audience.)*

JOEY. Help! Lion Tamer! Help!

*(LION has cornered JOEY. Just in the nick of time LION TAMER—one of the ENSEMBLE—chases after LION with net. RINGMASTER helps LION TAMER capture the LION. ALAN and LION TAMER put LION back into box.)*

JOEY. Oh, thank you, both! *(Hands ALAN back wand.)* I think I'll stick to coin tricks from now on. I'll let you do all the big tricks, Amazing.

ALAN. If you leave my ring, I can start my act. *(Motions to theater audience.)* They just can't wait any longer to see my incredible act.

JOEY. I'll go sit down.

ALAN. Please do. *(To ALISON.)* Ready, dearest?

ALISON. I've been ready for hours! You get no dessert tonight.

JOEY. Come on, you two. The show must go on!

RINGMASTER. Now, ladies and gentlemen, boys and girls, Joey's Circus is proud to present that astonishing artist of magic—

ALISON. That bonehead of a husband.

RINGMASTER. Amazing Alan!
ALAN. Thank you. *(Sings.)*

**(SONG #5: "MAGIC")**

**HERE'S SOME MYSTERY FOR YOU,**
**DARK AND DIFFICULT TO DO.**
**WATCH LIKE HAWKS AND YOU WILL SEE**
**NO ONE'S HALF AS GOOD AS ME!**

*(He repeats this verse, with ALISON adding lines as follows.)*

ALAN.
**HERE'S SOME MYSTERY FOR YOU.**

ALISON.
**HOW ABOUT SOME OTHER DAY?**

ALAN.
**DARK AND DIFFICULT TO DO.**

ALISON.
**FOR AWKWARD ALAN, ANYWAY!**

ALAN.
**WATCH LIKE HAWKS AND YOU WILL SEE**

ALISON.
**HIM DO A SILLY LITTLE TRICK**

ALAN.
**NO ONE'S HALF AS GOOD AS ME.**

ALISON.

**AT MAKING AUDIENCES SICK!**

ALAN.

**HERE I HAVE SOME SHINY RINGS;**
**ONE, TWO, THREE.**

ALISON.

**NOTICE HOW HE ALWAYS SINGS,**
**OUT OF KEY?**

ALAN.

**WATCH THEM JOIN INTO A CHAIN, MAGIC'LLY**

ALISON.

**THERE'S A PEANUT WHERE HIS BRAIN, OUGHT TO BE**

BOTH.

**ABARA CADABARA, PRESTO, CHANGE-O,**
**HOCUS POCUS DOMINOCUS, ALAKAZAM…**

ALAN.

**VISIBLY BEFORE YOUR EYES,**
**RINGS NOW LINK**

ALISON.

**ACTUALLY IT'S NO SURPRISE,**
**YOUR TRICKS STINK!**

ALAN.

**IN THE FIELD OF SORCERY, I'M A SCHOLAR**

ALISON.

**NOW SHOW THE FOLKS THE RINGS YOU'VE GOT 'ROUND THE COLLAR!**

*(Under music.)*

You'd better have a good reason for vanishing like that, Amazing. Here I am alone on the stage with your magic tricks, but no Alan...ARE YOU LISTENING TO ME? Answer me, Alan, you're acting as though you can't even hear me.

ALAN. What?

ALISON. I said...

*(ALAN puts his hands to his ears and pulls out a potato from each ear.)*

ALISON *(continuing)*. So you had potatoes in your ears, huh?

ALAN. Yes, potatoes in my ears.

ALISON. Good, we'll have french fries for dinner.

ALAN. Thanks, sweetie. *(Sings.)*

**YOU ARE CLEARLY AMAZED;**
**MAGIC SPIRITS HAVE BEEN RAISED!**
**AND SINCE I'M SO SUAVE AND SLICK**
**I SHALL DO ANOTHER TRICK!**

*(As before, ALISON adds her remarks to each line.)*

ALAN *(continuing)*.

**YOU ARE CLEARLY AMAZED**

ALISON.

**THAT HE CAN WALK AND TALK AT ONCE!**

ALAN.
**MAGIC SPIRITS HAVE BEEN RAISED**

ALISON.
**THEY LIKE TO FLOCK AROUND A DUNCE.**

ALAN.
**AND SINCE I'M SO SUAVE AND SLICK,**

ALISON.
**ON HIS BELLY THERE'S A WART!**

ALAN.
**I SHALL DO ANOTHER TRICK.**

ALISON.
**LET'S JUST HOPE IT'S MIGHTY SHORT!**

ALAN.
**HERE I HAVE A CABINET, LONG AND BRIGHT**

ALISON.
**FIGURED WHAT GOES IN IT YET?**
**YEP, YOU'RE RIGHT.**

ALAN.
**CUTE ASSISTANT ALISON, CLIMB INSIDE**

ALISON.
**THIS ONE IS A LOT OF FUN! (I JUST LIED.)**

BOTH.

**ABARA CADABARA, PRESTO CHANGE-O**
**HOCUS POCUS DOMINOCUS, ALAKAZAM.**

*(ALISON has climbed into the standard "sawing-a-lady-in-half" box. ALAN saws the box in two and separates the halves.)*

ALAN.

**THOUGH I SAWED HER CLEAN IN HALF,**
**SHE'S OKAY.**

ALISON *(her upper half singing from the box).*

**SURE, THAT'S PLENTY EASY FOR HIM TO SAY!**

ALAN.

**SEE, SHE STILL CAN WALK AND TALK,**
**BRIGHT AND PERKY.**

ALISON.

**FUNNY HOW HE CARVES ME UP,**
**BUT CAN'T SLICE TURKEY!**

ALISON. Really, Alan. After all these years, are those the best tricks you can do?

ALAN. What do you mean? I thought they were terrific!

ALISON. Can't you do anything more amazing? Why don't you do something spectacular...a real crowd-pleaser?

ALAN. A crowd-pleaser, eh?

ALISON. Yes. Let's see a trick that'll make people stand up and cheer!

ALAN. Actually, there *is* ONE trick that I could do. I'm sure the audience will like it…I know I will. I've been saving it for a special occasion.
ALISON. Well, come on, balloonhead, let's see it now!
ALAN. Now?
ALISON. Right this second!
ALAN. OK, here goes!

*(Music resumes.)*

BOTH.
**ABARA CADABARA, PRESTO CHANGE-O**
**HOCUS POCUS DOMINOCUS, ALAKAZAM!**

*(On "Alakazam," ALAN gestures mystically at the bewildered ALISON, who suddenly vanishes in a puff of smoke.)*

ALAN. That's the best trick I've ever done, if I do say so. And I do!

*(ALAN bows. ENSEMBLE applauds as lights dim out and spotlight shines on RINGMASTER.)*

RINGMASTER. Now, boys and girls, in the center ring, those crazy, zany and funny—clowns!

*(A small clown car enters. One at a time, CLOWNS come out of it. After they come out, they all sit around the ring with heads down. RINGMASTER is upset about this.)*

RINGMASTER. Ha, ha, ha, isn't this fun, everybody? I just love clowns. They're so funny. They make me laugh… Ha, ha, ha, hee, hee, hee. *(Without missing a beat, he drops his fake smile and continues.)* All right, what's going on here?

JOEY. Ringmaster, what's wrong with the clowns?

RINGMASTER. I don't know, but I'm going to find out. *(Moves to CLOWNS. JOEY follows.)* What's going on? You're supposed to be performing…entertaining the kids, clowning around, being funny.

CLOWN #1. We don't feel like it.

CLOWN #2. Yes. We're depressed.

CLOWN #3. And sad.

CLOWN #4. We don't feel like making people laugh.

CLOWN #5. We don't feel funny.

CLOWN #6. I want my mommy!

RINGMASTER. If you bozos don't stand up and start doing your bits, I'm going to have you fired.

CLOWN #1. Would you do that for us?

CLOWN #2. We'd appreciate it.

CLOWN #3. Yes. That would be awfully nice.

CLOWN #4. We don't want to be funny anymore.

CLOWN #5. No more yuck-yucks from us.

CLOWN #6. I want my mommy!

RINGMASTER. Well, then, we'll just move on to the next act. Ladies and gentlemen, boys and girls, those marvels of the Mediterranean, the—

JOEY. Wait! Let me talk to these clowns.

RINGMASTER. Go ahead! It's your circus…

*(CLOWNS start to cry.)*

RINGMASTER *(to audience)*. I've never seen clowns so sad, have you? *(After a response.)* Neither have I.

JOEY *(to CLOWNS)*. Excuse me, ah…I'm Joey…the B-O-S-S.

CLOWN #1 *(crying)*. How do you do?

CLOWN #6. You're not my mommy! *(Cries.)*

JOEY. Why are you all so down? Why don't you want to perform?

CLOWN #2. We're just sick and tired.

JOEY. Sick and tired of what?

CLOWN #3. Of always making people laugh. Nobody ever makes *us* laugh.

JOEY. What?

CLOWN #4. People all over the world go to see a clown to cheer them up. Who does a clown go to see?

JOEY. Well, I see your point.

CLOWN #5. We want a few laughs every once in a while.

CLOWN #6. So does my mommy!

JOEY. Excuse me just a second. *(Moves to RINGMASTER.)* Don't we have anybody in the circus to make these clowns laugh?

RINGMASTER. Nope. We can thrill them, scare them or enchant them, but to make them laugh? Only clowns can do that.

JOEY. Maybe there's another circus in town. Maybe we can get a clown from there to come here?

RINGMASTER. Good idea, but there's no other circus in town right now. Only yours.

JOEY. Then who will cheer them up?

RINGMASTER. Don't look at me. I think everything's terrible, remember?

JOEY. Then I guess…Ringmaster, get me a clown costume.

RINGMASTER. One clown costume coming up!

JOEY. And some makeup.

RINGMASTER. Sure. *(RINGMASTER signals for members of ENSEMBLE to bring JOEY a costume and makeup.)*

JOEY *(to CLOWNS)*. Listen, you sad-eyed creatures. Just you wait. Give me a little time and I'll have you rolling in the aisles with laughter.

CLOWN #1 *(sadly)*. Sure, you will.

CLOWN #2 *(even more sad)*. I'm laughing already.

CLOWN #3 *(very depressed)*. Trying to make us laugh. Now that's funny. *(A fake laugh.)*

*(During the following passage, JOEY is made up and dressed in a clown costume and ridiculously large shoes. RINGMASTER hands him a horn.)*

**(SONG #6: "MAKE YOU LAUGH")**

JOEY *(sings)*.

**HOW COULD YOU BE SO SAD**
**ON A DAY LIKE TODAY?**
**OUGHTA BE FEELING GLAD**
**COME ON, WHAT DO YOU SAY?**
**TELL YOU WHAT I CAN DO, THOUGH,**
**TO MAKE YOU LESS BLUE**
**I'LL BE A CLOWN MYSELF—**
**YES, THAT'S JUST WHAT I'LL DO!**

*(In tempo.)*

**I WANT TO MAKE YOU LAUGH AND SHOUT**
**I WANT TO GET THE DOLDRUMS OUT**
**I WANT TO HEAR YOU CHUCKLE,**

**BELIEVE ME, SOON YOUR LUCK'LL CHANGE!**
**I WANT TO SEE THOSE PEARLY WHITES**
**I WANT YOUR SMILE UP THERE IN LIGHTS**
**GIVE OUT A GIGGLE, OR START TO SQUEAL**
**AND PRETTY SOON HAPPY IS WHAT YOU'LL FEEL**

*(His "clowning" and the song are working. CLOWNS are smiling and laughing at him. They now join him in a few tricks. This should be a fast dance in which JOEY and the CLOWNS entertain the theater audience. CLOWNS now squirt RINGMASTER with seltzer bottles.)*

RINGMASTER *(laughing)*. I do believe, Joey, they're back to normal.

*(RINGMASTER wipes his face. CLOWNS run around audience maybe passing out balloons, shaking hands, doing tricks, etc. CLOWN #1 and CLOWN #2 are humorously fighting. CLOWN #1 chases all the OTHER CLOWNS around as CHASE MUSIC is played. CLOWNS join JOEY and RINGMASTER.)*

JOEY, RINGMASTER, CLOWNS *(sing)*.

**TURN THAT FROWN**
**UPSIDE DOWN**
**EVEN I CAN BE A CLOWN**
**DON'T BE GLUM,**
**START TO HUM**
**SOON A GRIN WILL COME!**
**I WANT TO SEE YOU FEELING GOOD**
**AND BEING SILLY AS YOU SHOULD**

**I WANT TO MAKE YOU CACKLE**
**GET WARMED UP AND THE KNACK'LL**
**COME BACKLE!**

**LAUGHTER CAN COME IN PEALS AND GALES**
**BURSTS AND GUFFAWS AND FITS AND WAILS**
**I WANT TO SEE YOUR LIGHTER HALF**
**I WANT TO MAKE YOU LAUGH!**

*(ENTIRE CAST now forms a kick-line for the song's Grand Finale.)*

ALL.

**WE WANT TO MAKE YOU LAUGH AND SHOUT**
**WE WANT TO GET THE DOLDRUMS OUT**
**WE WANT TO HEAR YOUR CHUCKLE**
**BELIEVE ME SOON YOUR LUCK'LL CHANGE**
**WE WANT TO SEE YOUR PEARLY WHITES**
**WE WANT YOUR SMILES UP THERE IN LIGHTS**
**WE WANT TO SEE YOUR LIGHTER HALF—**
**WE WANT TO MAKE YOU LAUGH!**

*(CLOWNS lose their formation and fall to the floor in hysterical giggles, gasps and guffaws. Eventually they gain clown-like composure and climb one by one back into the small car and hurry off. JOEY and RINGMASTER lead audience to waving goodbye. While JOEY quickly exits to get out of his clown costume, the RINGMASTER moves downstage into spotlight. The lights are somewhat dimmer. The mood has changed. A misty reprise of "Circus Time!" is being played on the piano. JOEY reenters.)*

RINGMASTER. Well, Joey, it's been a terrific day for our circus.

JOEY. So tell me, Ringmaster, what's the next act?

RINGMASTER. It's been fun and not so terrible.

JOEY. Oh, yes, it was fun! So the next act is?

RINGMASTER. You've been a terrific B-O-S-S. The best we've ever had.

JOEY. Thanks; now, introduce the next act please.

RINGMASTER. Joey, there's a time for joining the circus but there's a time for real life, too. We have to move on. We have a train waiting.

JOEY. You're leaving—already?

RINGMASTER. The circus never stays in one place very long.

JOEY. Oh, please don't go! Not yet. How about staying one more day? Please?

RINGMASTER. There are other cities to visit, other adventures to have, and other little boys and girls to entertain. You've been great, kiddo, but we have to pack up.

JOEY. Hey, I've got an idea. Let me go with you. You said I'm a good boss.

RINGMASTER. Can't do that, Joey.

JOEY. Why can't I come with you? Can't I join you forever?

RINGMASTER. No, Joey, your place isn't in the circus, at least not for now. You have a real life of thrills and adventures ahead of you.

JOEY. But...

RINGMASTER. Joey...

**(SONG #7: "FAREWELL/CIRCUS TIME! REPRISE")**

RINGMASTER *(sings).*
**IF YOU'LL BELIEVE IN MAGIC**
**AND NOT JUST WHAT YOU SEE**
**WE'LL BE HERE, IN YOUR MEMORIES**
**REAL AS CAN BE.**

JOEY.
**THE CIRCUS MUST BE LEAVING**
**I CAN'T BELIEVE IT'S TRUE**
**CAN'T YOU SEE,**
**I WON'T HAVE ANY FUN WITHOUT YOU?**

RINGMASTER.
**NOBODY LIVES IN THE THREE RINGS, JOEY.**
**THEY'RE JUST AN ILLUSION, TOO.**
**WE ARE JUST PEOPLE AND ANIMALS**
**WHO LIKE TO BRING MAGIC TO YOU.**

*(Various CIRCUS CHARACTERS move to JOEY.)*

FANGOONEE. Joey, you helped me overcome my fear of heights. Thank you.

JEANELLE. You figured out how we three sisters can remain good friends.

ELLIE & NELLIE. You've made us into a great duo.

JEANELLE. And you've given me a place to be myself.

*(JEANELLE plants a big wet kiss on JOEY's forehead. AMAZING ALAN and ALISON enter. ALISON has her head back in the cabinet she disappeared in earlier.)*

ALISON *(to ALAN)*. But, magic mouth, I'm still not speaking to you. *(ALAN tenderly kisses her hand. She smiles.)* Much.

*(ALAN reaches into the air and pulls out flowers.)*

ALAN. I promise no more disappearing acts. (*ALAN presents ALISON with the flowers.)*

ALISON. Oh, Alan.

CLOWN #4. Joey, you made us laugh again. Thanks.

CLOWN #5. You're a good clown.

CLOWN #6. My mommy thinks you're funny, too!

*(CLOWNS quickly squirt JOEY and laugh.)*

RINGMASTER. And Joey… *(Pauses, then puts his hand out.)*

JOEY *(shaking hands)*. Thank you, Ringmaster. Thank you, all. *(Sings.)*

**I KNOW YOU'VE GOT TO MOVE ON, MY FRIENDS,**
**THE CIRCUS TRAIN'S READY TO LOAD;**
**BUT LET'S SING IT OUT ONE MORE TIME—**
**LET'S SING IT ONCE FOR THE ROAD!**

*(THE ENTIRE CAST joins JOEY and RINGMASTER for the Finale.)*

ALL.

**CATCH THE TUNE**
**FEEL THE BEAT**
**IT'S THE CIRCUS PARADE**
**COMING DOWN THE STREET!**
**HANG ONTO YOUR HATS**

**FOR A THREE-RING SHOW—**
**THIS SPECTACULAR DAY**
**IS ALL FOR JOE!**

**STEP RIGHT UP**
**DON'T BE SHY**
**WE'LL MAKE SMILES APPEAR**
**AND CAUSE SPIRITS TO FLY!**
**WE'LL BUILD AN ILLUSION**
**ONE, TWO OR THREE**
**YOU'LL BE GLUED TO YOUR SEATS,**
**JUST WAIT AND SEE!**

*(CIRCUS MEMBERS stop singing. Music continues. All eyes are on JOEY as he suddenly spies his bathrobe still on the floor. JOEY realizes that it's time to grow up and be more responsible. He slowly picks up bathrobe and hangs it on the hook. CIRCUS MEMBERS all smile. JOEY too has learned something today.)*

ALL *(sing).*
**IT'S CIRCUS TIME FOR JOEY.**
**THE SUN IS SETTING SOON**
**WE'LL BE GONE**
**BUT WE KNOW YOU'LL REMEMBER THE TUNE**
**IT'S CIRCUS TIME FOREVER**
**IT'S CIRCUS TIME FOR YOU**
**IT'S CIRCUS TIME!**
**IT'S CIRCUS TIME!**
**IT'S CIRCUS TIME!**
**IT'S CIRCUS TIME TODAY!**

*(Unseen by anyone, RINGMASTER leaves his hat in Joey's bedroom. In a blaze of pageantry, the CIRCUS*

*leaves the stage. JOEY, enraptured by it all, is not watching them. Momentarily he turns, as though addressing the RINGMASTER, and finds that the circus is gone. He notices his set of circus dolls is arranged on the floor like they were in the opening.)*

MOTHER *(offstage)*. Joey!

*(JOEY quickly picks up circus dolls, quickly makes his bed, and puts dolls neatly back.)*

MOTHER *(offstage)*. Joey!
JOEY. Coming, Mom.
MOTHER *(offstage)*. Joey, it's dinnertime!

*(JOEY starts to leave room, takes glance back to see if everything is neatly put away. He spies RINGMASTER's hat. He picks it up. Wonderingly, he puts it on and proclaims.)*

JOEY. It's circus time!

*(JOEY runs out. Blackout.)*

**END OF PLAY**

# DIRECTOR'S NOTES

# DIRECTOR'S NOTES

# DIRECTOR'S NOTES

# DIRECTOR'S NOTES